ESSENTIAL [DK] FINANCE

INVESTING
BASICS

MARC ROBINSON

[DK]

DORLING KINDERSLEY

London • New York • Sydney • Delhi • Paris • Munich • Johannesburg

A DORLING KINDERSLEY BOOK

Editor Stephanie Rubenstein
Design and Layout Hedayat Sandjari
Photography Anthony Nex
Project Editor Crystal A. Coble
Project Art Editor Mandy Earey
DTP Designer Jill Bunyan
Content Consultant Stephanie Maloney
Photo Research Mark Dennis, Sam Ruston
Indexing Rachel Rice
Editorial Director LaVonne Carlson
Design Director Tina Vaughan
Publisher Sean Moore

First American Edition, 2000
2468109753

Published in the United States by
Dorling Kindersley Publishing, Inc.
95 Madison Avenue,
New York, New York 10016
See our complete catalog at
www.dk.com

Packaged by Top Down Productions
Copyright © 2000
Dorling Kindersley Publishing, Inc.
Text copyright © 2000 Marc Robinson

Dorling Kindersley Publishing, Inc. offers special discounts for
bulk purchases for sales promotions or premiums. Specific,
large quantity needs can be met with special editions, including
personalized covers, excerpts of existing guides, and corporate
imprints. For more information, contact Special Markets Dept.,
Dorling Kindersley Publishing, Inc., 95 Madison Ave., NY,
NY 10016; Fax: (800) 600-9098

Library of Congress Cataloging-in-Publication Data

Robinson, Marc, 1955-
    Investing basics / Marc Robinson -1st American ed.
        p.   cm.
    Includes index.
    ISBN 0-7894-6315-6
    1. Investments. 2.Finance, Personal. I. Title.

HG4521.R6642 2000
332.6–dc21   00-031495

Reproduced by Colourscan, Singapore
Printed by Wing King Tong, Hong Kong

CONTENTS

BASIC RISKS OF INVESTING

WAYS TO MANAGE RISK

UNDERSTANDING PERFORMANCE

STARTING OUT WITH CONFIDENCE

INTRODUCTION

Investing your money can be one of the most rewarding activities you do, or it can be one of the most unnerving. So much of investing is tied to our hopes and dreams, inhibitions and fears that it can be difficult separating the real from the imagined risks. The fact that the world of investing itself can be overwhelming drives many people from participating at all. Investing Basics is designed for you to easily grasp the relatively few basic elements that form the foundation of everything in investing. From this book, you will gain a clear understanding of setting goals, developing strategies, selecting the most appropriate investments, handling risks intelligently, using time wisely, and finding professionals to help when you need it. Most of all, Investing Basics will give you the confidence to be in control of your money as you aim toward a stable, comfortable future.

YOU CONTROL YOUR MONEY

The most important rule of investing is so simple, it's easy to be taken lightly: You decide what will happen with your money. What it can do for you is up to you.

WHAT TO DO WITH IT

The moment you receive money, you have to use it. Whether you can't let go of it, need to keep it close by, or can easily trust others to borrow it, you always have something to gain or lose. Here are the main choices.

---

1 You should understand what you're getting in return for giving up control of your money.

SPEND IT

You can buy things with it (always the crowd favorite).

STASH IT AT HOME

If you stash money at home, it's available any time and you won't lose it. But it's a sure way to lose money because inflation will slowly erode its buying power. Your job is to find ways to fight against that.

BANK IT

Banks want to borrow your money. By opening an account, you lend it to them until you need it. In return, you can have checks for quick access to your money and earn interest from a savings account or similar investment.

LEND IT

You can lend money by buying bonds (where the bond issuer repays lenders like you with interest). Government entities and companies borrow money for many reasons, such as improvements and research and development.

2 Investing your money should be about investing for a better life—for you or someone you care about.

BUY PUBLICLY OWNED COMPANIES

You can become a part owner of a company by buying shares of its stock. If the company does well, you might participate in the success. If it does poorly, you may lose money, just as any company owner would.

PAY THE PROS TO DO IT FOR YOU

Mutual funds are professional money managers for the masses. You decide what you want your money to do, then select a fund that aims for that objective. The profits and losses are yours, minus the fees.

You can buy a home or other real estate. You gain or lose according to how the property value fluctuates.

GAMBLE

You can roll the dice, buy lottery tickets, or play any game of chance and hope to make a profit—or risk losing it all. You could also invest in stocks and bonds without knowing what you're doing.

SOME BASIC PRINCIPLES

*T*o *invest means to use something in a way that will give you more value in the future. Deciding to invest means thinking of your time and money as a tool for achieving some worthwhile goals.*

WHAT ARE SECURITIES?

Securities are tools created for people to either share ownership or to lend money. They're packaged according to strict government standards. When a company wants the public to share its ownership (going public), it's required by law to package shares of stock as a security, file the package for government approval, and offer it to the public according to very specific rules. When a company or governmental body wants to borrow money from the public, it must follow other, similar procedures.

MONEY WORKS FOR YOU

If you owned a company, you would have employees working for you. Think of your money that way. The more money you send out in the world to work for you, the more money you can accumulate to produce wealth for you.

INVESTING CHOICES

As an investor, your job is to find opportunities to use (invest) your money. For example, you can:

- Be a lender or an owner;
- Keep the money close to you or let others use it for longer periods with more control. The longer you let someone use your money, the more you should be paid for that use. The more risk someone puts your money under, the more they should be willing to pay you for trusting them with those risks.

BUY LOW, SELL HIGH

You usually can't tell when an investment is high-priced and ready for a fall, or vice versa. But you can keep in mind that:

- Professionals often recognize a high price and sell a security before the general public reaches the same conclusion, leaving average investors as the ones to carry the losses;
- The higher the price goes, the more people may become fearful and begin to sell;
- People tend to look at past performance instead of future prospects, and therefore, often end up buying high and selling low;
- It's more difficult for something to rise than for it to fall, which means that prices are generally capable of falling much faster than they rise.

GUARD YOUR MONEY FROM LOSSES

It's a lot easier to lose money than it is to make more. For example, percentages are misleading. If you lose 50% of your money it will take a 100% gain to get back to where you started, not a 50% gain.

3 Investing is a matter of deciding how much trust or faith you have in the promises being made to you.

A DEFINITION OF SAVING

Over a lifetime, the wealthy often become wealthy because they follow these two simple rules. First, they save, meaning that they spend less than they earn. Second, they use credit wisely and don't become overextended in debt.

Preparing Yourself for Wealth

A financial plan doesn't have to be perfect. You can always adjust it as you learn. Every goal—and every plan to achieve that goal—is as individual as the person who makes it.

4 Every investment plan focuses on the four basic questions mentioned here.

Where Do You Want to Be?

Set clear goals for how you want to use your money. A goal is what you want to achieve in your life. The money you accumulate will be used to help you get there.

For example, your goal could be a house, a car, a comfortable retirement, an amount of money by a certain date, an income stream for your family when you die or if you can't work. It could be food for the local shelter every Thanksgiving for the next ten years, or to help find a cure for a disease.

Now you're giving the concept of investing some shape and definition. You have a sense of how much money you will need, and how long before you will need it.

How Will You Get There?

Set your strategy according to what you want to accomplish.
Protection. Do you want to protect what you already have saved? For example, you've saved enough for a down payment on a home. Now it's time to invest in something safe until you find the right home.
Income. Do you want to earn income? Maybe you need just enough money to afford a small vacation without spending the savings you already have.
Growth. Do you need to accumulate a large amount of money to be able to pay for a major goal in your life? How much, for example, would you like to be able to contribute to your child's college education?

WHAT WILL GET YOU THERE?

You've gauged how much you will need. You've seen how much time you have to reach the goal. Maybe you need to earn a lot in a short time. You might, instead, need to earn an amount that seems appropriate for the amount of time. You might even be lucky enough to have plenty of time to achieve your goal. With this awareness, you can narrow the field of possible investments by determining which ones have at least the potential to achieve your goal within your time frame.

> **5** Time plays a critical role in every investment decision. Consider it carefully.

WHAT COULD STOP YOU?

Once you've assessed your goals, understood the basic strategies, and looked at what investments might get you there on time, you can look at the more predictable outcomes of investments and the potential risks from a more analytical, rather than emotional, perspective.

For example, the risk of losing some money may be relatively minor compared to the risk of not reaching your goal. If, on the other hand; the risk of a particular investment seems too high, you will have to consider how far short of your goal you would be willing to fall. Knowing that, you could see whether other investments, or combinations of investments, might offer an acceptable level of risk.

BASIC INVESTING STRATEGIES

While investment strategies have a reputation for being quite complex, the cornerstone strategies are simple, and most are used by even the most advanced investors.

THREE UNIVERSAL STEPS

You buy. You hold. You sell. These three activities are what it takes to be an investor; the fundamental elements of every investment strategy.

HOLDING IS THE KEY

How long you hold an investment can affect every other aspect of your strategy. For example, if your strategy is protection, you would choose an investment with the best potential safety during your planned holding period. For an income strategy, you would look for an investment that can provide the income you need during your holding period. For a growth strategy, you would look for an investment with the potential to rise in price in accordance with your time frame.

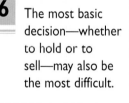

6 The most basic decision—whether to hold or to sell—may also be the most difficult.

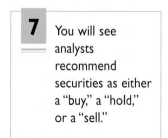

7 You will see analysts recommend securities as either a "buy," a "hold," or a "sell."

MARKET TIMING OR LONG-TERM INVESTING?

If you try to time the market, you might miss the best days. This table shows what would have happened to a short-term trader who, in trying to time the market, ended up missing just a few critical days in the last 10 years. For example, the trader would have lost over 4% by missing just ten days of the last ten years.

INVESTMENT PERIOD 1989-1999	S&P 500 INDEX ANNUALIZED RETURN*
If you invested for all 2, 527 days	15.7%
If you missed the 10 best days	11.5%
If you missed the 20 best days	8.7%
If you missed the 30 best days	6.3%
If you missed the 40 best days	4.1%

* This information assumes that assets, when not invested in stocks, earned interest at average Treasury Bill rates. Returns are through 2/28/99. The S&P 500 Index measures the performance of 500 large company stocks. Source: Prudential Investments.

EMOTIONAL SELLING AND DAY TRADING

Some investors trade on emotions or try to beat the market through quick trades for profits. Online trading and low commissions have made *day trading* attractive to individual investors. Try to make short-term decisions that are based on the goals and strategies you've planned for that money. Make sure your money is doing the job you planned for it to do.

HOLDING SHORT-TERM: TRADING

This is called *timing* the market to buy low and sell high soon after. Successful trading takes a lot of close attention, courage, and luck. It may also be expensive, because you might pay a fee every time you trade and pay capital gains taxes if you profit.

If, for example, you pay a 5% sales charge for a mutual fund, earn 8% interest, then sell, you would only have 3% left. Or, if you buy 100 shares of stock at $10 (for $1,000) and pay a $35 commission (3.5%), the price of your stock would have to go up 3.5% just to break even.

HOLDING LONG-TERM: INVESTING

If you take a longer-term approach—if your goals are bigger and more far-reaching—there is probably no need to buy and sell quickly. You can find a use for your money that coincides with your longer-term goals, then give it time to do what you expect it to do without worrying whether the price falls occasionally. This is the strategy most financial professionals recommend, particularly for people who want their money to grow over time.

THREE MAIN STRATEGIES

*B*eing *a successful investor doesn't necessarily mean making a lot of money. Like choosing the proper clothes for the occasion, the right strategy is the one that suits your goal. Whether you're rich or poor, a beginner or an expert, there are three basic strategies in investing.*

TO PROTECT

One strategy is simply to hold onto what you've already saved. This means you need to make safety your top priority.

With money, safety doesn't translate into a do-nothing approach. To the contrary, doing nothing with money or keeping it in a no-interest account allows inflation to erode its buying power until it has less value than when you started. For protection, therefore, investors try to keep close control over their money by lending it for short periods to borrowers who have proven, reliable reputations.

Since borrowers can't do much with money they have to repay quickly, they shouldn't pay much interest. That's an acceptable trade-off for investors who consider an investment to be successful if it earns enough to offset inflation and protects their money until they need it

TO EARN INCOME

The second main strategy is to make income the top priority. This means earning an income that will not only outpace inflation, but provide some additional money. Investing to earn income is for people who want to receive regular installments of money, or want at least some predictability in the amount they can earn, or when they will earn it.

Investors with income as a main strategy allow others to use their money for longer periods of time than they would allow if they were protecting their money. In return, they expect to be better compensated for taking the added risk that is a by-product of having less control.

8 Be suspicious of any investment that is supposedly designed to meet all three strategies.

9 Many professionals believe asset allocation is the most critical factor in investment performance.

TO GROW MORE

The third main strategy is to list your top priority as using your money to grow more money— even, in some cases, as much money as you can. A growth strategy requires investors to give up the most control and a significant level of predictability about the success of the strategy.

In return for unpredictability and loss of control, growth investors expect to be more highly compensated than protection or income investors, and within a reasonable time period. If the compensation—in the form of a stock price rise, for example— doesn't materialize, the investors can sell and take back as much of their money as they can.

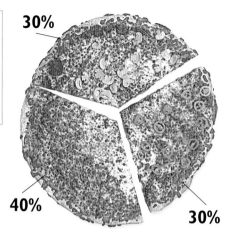

30%

40%

30%

▲ ASSET ALLOCATION IS CRUCIAL

There are three main asset classes that coincide with the three main investment strategies. Dividing or allocating the available money among the asset classes (for example, a 30%-30%-40% allocation model) is considered a crucial part of any investment plan. Each asset class is better suited for a particular strategy than the other two. Investors typically allocate certain percentages of their investment dollars to each asset class. Cash equivalents is the asset class most used by investors with a protective strategy (see page 20 for more). Fixed income, typically bonds, is the asset class most used by investors with an income strategy (see page 24 for more). Equities, typically stocks, is the asset class most used by investors with a growth strategy (see page 26 for more).

COMBINING STRATEGIES

Some investments are designed for two strategies. For example, balanced mutual funds are designed for both income and growth. Like buying a sleeper sofa that isn't as good as a bed or as good as a sofa, you may sacrifice some of one strategy's potential in exchange for having dual requirements.

THE TWO SIMPLEST WAYS TO GROW MONEY

The simple act of not touching your money allows the easiest, most powerful strategy ever devised for making money—compounding— to work its magic. It also helps you save on taxes. This is the most valuable lesson in investing: The more money you have the faster it can grow. In other words, as money accumulates, the pace of its growth accelerates. Even though it's natural to want to spend some of your profit, if you have a long time before you need the money, you may want to let it accumulate instead and grow faster as it does. Here's how compounding works.

THE POWER OF COMPOUNDING

It takes discipline to reinvest earnings instead of spending them. Notice that after a few years the strategy begins to pay off as the growth accelerates faster than during the earlier years

Hands off
Say, for example, you start by investing $1,200 a year in a mutual fund that earns 8% a year. Every year, you reinvest earnings so that they also earn 8% interest. After twenty years, you have almost $46,000.

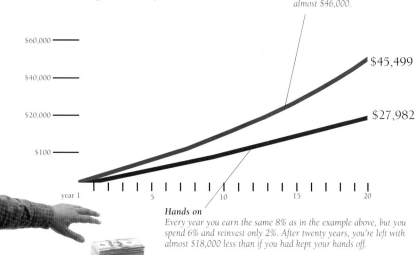

$45,499

$27,982

$60,000

$40,000

$20,000

$100

year 1   5   10   15   20

Hands on
Every year you earn the same 8% as in the example above, but you spend 6% and reinvest only 2%. After twenty years, you're left with almost $18,000 less than if you had kept your hands off.

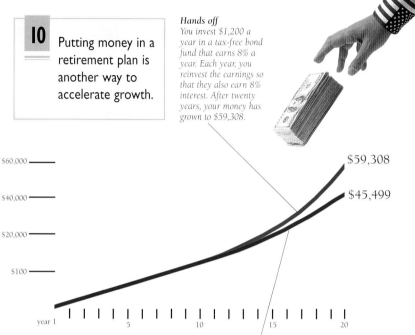

| **10** | Putting money in a retirement plan is another way to accelerate growth. |

Hands off
You invest $1,200 a year in a tax-free bond fund that earns 8% a year. Each year, you reinvest the earnings so that they also earn 8% interest. After twenty years, your money has grown to $59,308.

$60,000 ——
$40,000 ——
$20,000 ——
$100 ——

year 1   5   10   15   20

$59,308
$45,499

THE POWER OF REDUCING TAXES

A major part of any plan to grow money involves reducing taxes. In fact, local, state, and federal governments encourage you to use your money in certain socially desirable ways by letting you skip paying taxes. For example, if you buy your state's municipal bonds (lend money to your state or local government), you won't pay federal income tax on the earnings. If you lend money to the federal government (buy Treasuries), you won't pay state and local income tax. If reinvesting earnings makes money grow faster, reinvesting all your earnings—in short, avoiding taxes—will accelerate growth even more.

Hands on
You invest the same $1,200 and earn the same 8% as above, but because you're not investing tax-deferred or tax-free, every year you pay a 28% tax on earnings. After twenty years, you end up with nearly $14,000 less than had you kept the government's hands off.

| **11** | Automatic reinvestment plans are another way to keep your hands off. |

17

Finding a Match for Your Money

Once you know your goals, you can look for investments that at least will give you a chance to reach those goals. Keep in mind that institutions trying to attract your money have different purposes. It's up to you to understand those purposes and to see whether they match your own. In short, you may want to match the promise of an investment with your own needs and look for compatibility. Here are a few choices to help you get started.

Small Companies

Small companies are usually looking to expand and grow. That may mean investing more in research and development, establishing a new product line, or other similar uses. Typically, they reinvest all of their profits—if they have any—back into the business instead of distributing them to shareholders.

People who buy stock in small companies aren't looking for income. They believe that the companies will grow and, consequently, make their shares of stock more valuable over time.

Personal ads

Young, aggressive stock seeks cash with same qualities for fast-paced relationship. Nothing heavy. Long-term commitment possible but not necessary. Photo please.

Long-term

Solid, secure stock wants cash of same for long-term relationship that pays all kinds of dividends. I'm dependable, you're loyal and loving but beyond infatuation. No kids please.

Large Companies

Companies that have been around for a while tend to provide more stability by having established product lines and distribution systems. Some have products with consistent, dependable sales even in unfavorable economic climates. Many earn enough profits to pay a portion to their stockholders.

People who buy these kinds of stock are often looking for slow, steady increases in share prices, with the added benefit of a little extra income.

SHORT-TERM LOANS

Many companies and governmental entities borrow money for short periods to manage cash flow, cover operating costs, or meet other short-term expenses. They will pay some interest and return your money within anywhere from one day to a year. The longer they keep it, the higher an interest rate you should expect them to pay.

People who want to keep their money readily accessible and safe tend to make short-term loans in investments such as a money market account (see page 20 for more details).

INTERMEDIATE AND LONG-TERM LOANS

Many companies and government entities have long-term goals that require financing. For example, companies may need money for new plants, offices, or technologies. Governments may need to build bridges or provide other community services. Typically, the longer they will want to use your money, the higher the interest they will be willing to pay to get the loan.

People who make longer-term loans usually want predictable income at higher rates than are available from making short-term loans.

12 Investing is a matter of deciding how much trust or faith you have in the promises being made to you.

HIGH RISK LOANS

Some institutional borrowers have difficulty attracting lenders. They may possibly have a poor record of repaying other loans. Maybe the purpose of the loan is itself a high risk venture. The money they borrow from investors may even go to pay off another loan. So to attract lenders, these borrowers must pay higher interest to make the potential income worth the risks. *Junk bonds*, are one form of high risk borrowing.

13 Successful investing is dependent upon matching your investments with your goals.

wild side

You like to live for the thrill of high returns. I'm a bond dangerously that promises a bumpy ride and lots of payoffs while it lasts. Can we make it all the way to the end together?

INVESTMENT CHOICES

Your investments reflect your decisions about how others can use your money. Be sure you can accept those uses. With that in mind here are the main types of investments.

CASH AND CASH EQUIVALENTS

Since one strategy is to protect what you've already saved, there are investments designed with safety as the top priority. By investing in securities from an asset class called cash equivalents, you try to protect your money and earn a little income at the same time.

WHAT ARE CASH EQUIVALENTS?

They are securities that let you keep your money close and safe by lending it for very short periods (a day to a year) to borrowers with reliable reputations. Investments designed for protection are called cash equivalents because in practice, they're designed to be almost as safe as cash.

THE CONCEPT OF LIQUIDITY

The faster you can get your money from an investment, the more *liquid* it is considered to be.

WHY USE THEM?

Many experts recommend keeping on hand at least six months worth of income for emergency situations (like losing a job). You may also choose to invest in cash equivalents if you're close to the time when you will be using the money. For example, you may have enough for a down payment on a home and don't want to risk losing it.

MONEY MARKET FUNDS

These are similar to savings accounts except that your money is pooled with other customers into one large sum. The money is then loaned to businesses for a short time, usually a week or less and sometimes overnight.

Money market funds are considered one of the safest investments. The interest earned is shared by all the customers and the bank takes a small fee for its efforts. Bank money market funds are federally insured. Money market mutual funds usually have private insurance, which has historically been very safe but isn't as safe as federal insurance.

SAVINGS ACCOUNTS

These are loans made to your bank with no time limits. You have the right to withdraw your money at any time. The bank lends your money to individuals or businesses and pays a portion of the interest it earns to you. While you earn some income from a savings account, it's designed mainly to protect what you already have. The interest you earn is among the lowest of any investment and the income is taxable, reducing your income even further. Savings accounts are federally insured up to $100,000.

CERTIFICATES OF DEPOSIT (CDs)

These loans to your bank are similar to savings accounts except that they have specific time limits. You agree to let the bank use your money for a period of time and pay you interest in return. When the time is up, you can either renew the loan (*roll it over*), withdraw it, or use it in another way at the bank. The longer you agree to let the bank use your money, the higher the rate of interest you can earn. The amount you keep is reduced by the taxes you will have to pay on the amount you've earned.

U.S. TREASURY BILLS

These are loans to the U.S. government for ninety days or less. This is the safest investment because repayment is guaranteed by the U.S. government itself. Treasuries offer another benefit that increases your income: they're exempt from state and local taxes so you keep more of your earnings.

14 Many investors use cash equivalents as temporary *parking places* until they're ready to use the money for something else.

LENDING MONEY: BONDS

*W*hen you buy fixed income securities, typically bonds,
you're lending money to earn some income. The borrower
might be a corporation or a state or federal government.

WHY INVEST IN BONDS?

Buying bonds reflects a decision to make income a higher priority
than protection. How much more of a priority is still a matter of
degree you can control.

1. MONEY IS NEEDED

Here's an example. A city may need to raise money to build, renovate, have operating money, or simply to pay off other debts. It hires an investment banker to help. The banker helps determine how much money it will need, how long it will need to repay the lenders (the investors), and the lowest interest rate it could get away paying and still attract enough interest from investors. A municipal bond offering is created, and the city is named as the municipal bond issuer.

2. FLOATING AN OFFER

The investment banker floats an offer to the public (tests it) to see if it can sell enough bonds at it's terms to raise all the money. If it can, everything moves ahead. If it can't, it may either reprice (determine a new interest rate and other terms) and try again, or withdraw the offering.

3. INVESTORS BUY

This is where you come In. Say you and other investors decide to invest. In effect, you're saying, "I'll lend you money. I'm willing to accept your promise to repay my loan plus interest, by the specific date, according to the terms in your offer." For example, you may buy several twenty-year bonds for $1,000 each. The city will be expected to pay a fixed interest rate of 6% ($60) every year, in four annual installments, for twenty years.

15 You can sell a bond at any time and take a profit or loss, apart from any interest you have earned.

4. WHAT IF INTEREST RATES DROP?

If interest rates drop, new bond issuers will enter the market selling new bonds with lower interest rates than yours. That will make your bonds more valuable. You could decide to sell your bonds. There will probably be others willing to buy. If you do sell, you can demand a profit (called a premium) because the bond pays more than the going rate. For example, if new bonds are being issued at 4%, buyers might agree to pay you $1,090 a bond for your 6% bonds. You would earn a $90 profit on each bond, and they would replace you as the new lenders. Now it would be their turn to receive interest payments and assume the risks of lending to this particular borrower.

5. WHAT IF INTEREST RATES RISE?

If rates rise, the reverse of #4 would occur. Your 6% bonds would be less valuable because investors could do better than 6% by buying new bonds. If the going rate for newly issued bonds is 8% you may be forced to sell at a discount (for example, $920) to entice potential buyers. You would have earned the interest up to the point of selling, but you would also take a loss of $80 on the original investment. (The bond cost $1,000. You sold it for $920. The difference is $80.)

6. MATURITY: THE LOAN ENDS

After twenty years, time is up on the loan. Every owner of these bonds at this time is paid $1,000 for each one, no matter when they bought the bond or at what price. For example, the person who paid you $920 a bond would now receive $1,000, or an $80 profit per bond, in addition to the interest earned.

THINK LIKE A LENDER

You may be "investing" in a bond, but you should still think like someone lending money to someone else. Here's what to consider.

The amount. Many bonds are initially sold in units of $1,000, called *par value*. After that, trading occurs at whatever prices the market will bear.

Issuer. This is the borrower. Check out the firm's or agency's reputation and the bond's quality rating. This is the best way to gauge your chances of being fully repaid with interest.

Yield. The amount you earn, based on the price you pay for the bond.

Maturity. When the loan is due. You don't have to stay until the end. You can sell the bonds at any time to anyone willing to take your place as the lender.

Call feature. A prepayment option. Some issuers reserve the right to *call* the bonds, which means they can prepay the entire loan and end it.

DURATION ▼

Duration is the term used to describe the time left until a bond matures (the loan ends). This tells you how long until the original investment is returned and you realize a gain or loss.

TYPES OF BONDS

T*he varieties of bonds abound, created to meet all kinds of investing strategies—and all kinds of borrowing needs. Each type offers different advantages and disadvantages.*

U.S. GOVERNMENT BONDS

There are three general groups of U.S. government securities:

- Treasury bills, bonds, and notes;
- Federal agency issue bonds, notes, and certificates;
- U.S. savings bonds.

These bonds are nearly risk-free, so they usually offer fairly low interest rates. This makes them attractive to conservative investors. The interest generated by federal government securities is exempt from state and local income taxes.

ZERO COUPON BONDS

Zeroes are corporate, municipal, or treasury bonds that pay no annual interest (*coupon rate* is another term for interest rate; so a zero coupon bond is a bond that pays zero interest). Investors buy zeroes at deep discounts and then redeem them for full value at maturity. The profit on that difference in value replaces the annual interest. Zeroes allow you to buy more bonds for your money. Be careful, though, you may be taxed annually as if you earn interest even if you don't actually receive the interest. Ask your financial or tax advisor.

MORE THINKING LIKE A LENDER

It might be helpful to ask certain questions when you're considering investing some of your money in bonds.

- How much should I lend?
- Is the borrower creditworthy?
- Will I earn enough interest on my loan?
- When and how will I be paid?

CONVERTIBLE BONDS

Some corporate bonds are convertible, meaning they can be exchanged at a specified time for a specific number of shares of stock held by the company that issued the bond. You earn income and can still benefit as an owner if the stock price rises. Convertible bonds usually are less volatile in price swings than the common stock from the same company, possibly because investors have:

- The added benefit of earning regular income and therefore may be less inclined to sell;
- Priority for repayment over common stockholders in cases where the company goes bankrupt.

Short-Term Fixed Income Funds

By investing in these funds, you pool your money with other investors. The fund manager then lends your money for somewhat longer periods than in money market funds.

Generally, the strategy is to minimize the possibility of loss due to a borrower failing to repay. Many people investing for protection consider the added risks of these funds to be minimal and worth the opportunity to earn a little more interest.

16 Capital gains on a bond are taxable even if the interest on the bond is tax-free.

Corporate Bonds

Corporations often finance major projects by issuing bonds rather than selling stock, primarily because of tax regulations. Although most state laws require corporations to pay bondholders before paying short-term creditors, experts recommend that investors consider the following factors when planning a corporate bond investment:
- The financial quality of the company;
- The company's current profitability;
- The company's long-term financial outlook and stability.

17 Every year, over 100 bond-issuing corporations file for bankruptcy and cause their bondholders to lose money.

Municipal Bonds

Municipal bonds are long-term loans made to state and local governments to finance public improvement projects. Income is usually paid semi-annually, and if the bond was issued in your home state, the interest you earn is free from federal, state, and any local income tax. That means you keep more of what you earn—but it also means that the interest rates are lower than taxable bonds. It's important to check your tax rate and see whether you would earn more after taxes from a municipal or a corporate bond. There are two main kinds of municipal bonds:
- General obligation bonds, which raise money the government may use for any purpose it wishes;
- Revenue bonds, which raise money for specific projects such as building a new power plant or highway. The interest is paid from project revenues.

OWNING BUSINESSES: STOCKS

M*any companies are owned by people like you. To go public, a company divides its ownership into equal shares and sells them to the public. If you own its stock, you share in the success if it does well, and in the failure if it doesn't. In short, most people buy stock to let their fortunes ride with the fortunes of the company.*

1. A COMPANY GOES PUBLIC

The owners of a small private company need to raise money to stay competitive. They could continue to borrow, but the best way to raise enough money to meet their goals is to ask many people to invest in the company's future. The company hires an investment banker to take them public. The banker looks at the company's assets, debts, and profit potential, then calculates how many shares to offer and at what opening price. It's a balancing act. There shouldn't be too many shares, which could flood the market, or too few, which would make shares in short supply. The price should also not be so high to discourage investors or too low to fall short of the shares' fair value.

2. INVESTORS BUY IN

On opening day, the shares enter the market as an initial public offering (IPO). The investment banker pays the company for all the shares and then resells the shares to the public. The once-private owners are now sharing ownership with the public.

3. THE COMPANY BENEFITS

The company doesn't directly receive more money from the stock trading. Still, it benefits from a rising price because ownership in the company becomes more valuable and says the company is succeeding. Most of all, rising prices let the management borrow more money, using the value of its stock as collateral.

5. THE COMPANY PROGRESS

The company's management may reinvest its earnings until it believes it can share some profits with shareholders and still remain fully competitive. Eventually, they may begin paying a dividend (distributing profits) for every share owned. By this time, you may have sold your stock and may no longer be a shareholder, but others are shareholders, and trading will continue to go around and around as long as the company remains in business.

4. INVESTORS FOLLOW THE PROGRESS

Research professionals analyze the company and distribute reports to the public. Every day, people who want to become owners negotiate prices with people who want to sell their shares and get out. Over the long term, the stock price will reflect how well a company is performing in its business. Over shorter terms, though, stock price is affected mainly by one thing: supply and demand. If a few people want to sell, but a lot of people want to own the stock, the sellers will drive up their asking price to see just how much the buyers are willing to pay. The price will rise as long as there are people willing to pay higher prices to become an owner. The reverse is also true: if shares become hard to sell, the price will fall until it reaches a level where people are willing to buy.

THINK LIKE AN OWNER

Stockholders can earn profits in two ways:
● Through distributions of a company's profits, called dividends;
● From an increase in the price of a share of the company's stock.

TYPES OF STOCKS

There are many types of stocks. Unlike bonds, these types aren't created to meet an investing need. Instead, they reflect the types of companies in the world and their various stages of development.

COMMON STOCK

The fundamental form of ownership in a public company is the common stock. Owners of common stock bear the primary burden of business risk but also receive the lion's share of any success.

There are many different ways to group stocks, depending on who is doing the grouping. Generally, a stock is first looked at as either a growth stock (shareholders are looking mainly for price appreciation), or an income stock (shareholders own it to earn income from its dividends). Second, stocks are commonly referred to using names based on the life cycle of the company.

Speculative stocks. These are the start-up, or relatively new companies who have not yet established themselves in their product or service market. They may also be companies in high risk businesses, such as the Internet, biotechnology, and a number of other highly competitive and money-intensive industries.

Growth stocks. These are companies that have moved beyond the phase of uncertainty but still have a lot of room to grow. The more and faster they grow, the more stock price movement investors can expect to see.

Value stocks. These are well-established companies with histories of consistent earnings and growth.

Some investors buy stocks of well-known companies for the dividends first, and for the price appreciation potential second.

BLUE CHIP STOCKS ▼
This title is reserved for only the most established, best-known companies. They have long, steady histories of solid growth and earnings as well as a strong foothold in their customer bases.

PREFERRED STOCK

Some companies offer a separate class of stock called preferred stock. These stocks are designed to be attractive to income-oriented investors by paying higher dividends than their counterparts—the common stock issued by the company. The preferred status means, among other things, that if the company goes bankrupt, the preferred stockholders would be in a position to recoup their money before shareholders of common stock.

THE CONCEPT OF *UNDERVALUED*

Some companies' stock prices may be lower than the actual value of the company due to investor perceptions. For example, the company may have had some negative news that they've overcome, but investors have not yet recognized the change.

THINGS TO KNOW

- Some stocks offer both growth and income potential. A strong, well-established company for example, could be in a booming industry with a lot of growth potential, and also pay attractive dividends.

- Utilities have long been called income stocks because they historically have paid high dividends and their prices have moved in narrow ranges. Some states are deregulating their power companies, which means the competition may affect the companies' needs to reinvest the profits rather than pay them as dividends. You may even find some historically stable utilities acting more like growth stocks.

- A decade ago, stock prices were considered high if they were twenty or thirty times the company's earnings per share. Today, many Internet stocks, among others, can sell for several hundred dollars a share yet have absolutely no earnings per share—a perfect example of how prices are based on investors' hopes of future earnings.

GROUPING BY SIZE

Companies are generally grouped into one of three main categories based on their overall market value. The market value is the price of the stock multiplied by the number of shares in the market, commonly called *market capitalization.*

Large-cap. These have over $5 billion in market value;

Mid-cap. These have a market value between $1 billion and $5 billion;

Small-cap. These have a market value of under $1 billion.

MUTUAL FUNDS

If you lack the time, interest, or ability to invest on your own, you can join millions of others who give their money to one of thousands of professional money managers who run mutual funds. Each fund pools all of their clients' money and invests it according to the general goals and strategies of the fund. By joining forces with many other hard workers who don't want to manage their own money, you gain power to do more than you can do alone.

THEY CREATE LEVERAGE

Mutual funds let you use your money as though you were a large investor. The combined resources of many small investors give you enough money to purchase more shares and more securities. Buying in large quantities can also lead to better prices and reduced commissions. Most of all, combining forces with other investors gives you the ability to afford to pay for the services of professional money management.

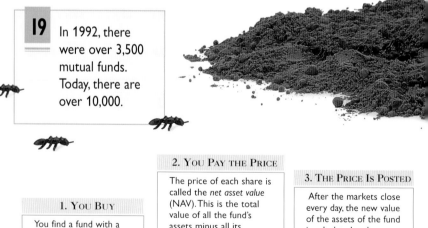

19 In 1992, there were over 3,500 mutual funds. Today, there are over 10,000.

1. YOU BUY

You find a fund with a strategy that's in line with your own. You buy some shares in that fund.

2. YOU PAY THE PRICE

The price of each share is called the *net asset value* (NAV). This is the total value of all the fund's assets minus all its liabilities, then divided by the total number of shares issued by the fund.

3. THE PRICE IS POSTED

After the markets close every day, the new value of the assets of the fund is calculated and a new NAV is posted for investors to see.

FINDING YOUR FUND

Every fund lists a fund objective that corresponds to the three main uses of money: protection, income, and growth (or a combination). This helps you find the right fund for your needs and helps each fund's managers make decisions based on what their clients (like you) expect of them. Different funds may use different strategies to try to achieve their objectives. Marketing brochures will give you a sense of these strategies. Some managers make decisions strictly from mathematical models. Others study a company's business in detail.

THINGS TO KNOW

- Give your money to a pro, and it will be managed using the tools of a pro. Many funds are only required to invest 65% of the money in assets central to the fund's objective. The other 35% is often used to push for higher returns or limit risks using options, futures, foreign securities, currencies, and a list of other sophisticated investments.

- Unit Investment Trusts are sold in units of $1,000. Unlike mutual funds, they hold a fixed portfolio of securities instead of trading. That makes costs lower, although your money can't shift out of bad performers or into good ones. They also usually expire after a certain date.

4. YOU SHARE THE COSTS

You share the costs of the fund with all other shareholders—the managers' salaries, operating expenses, legal and accounting costs, promotions, etc.— based on your percentage of ownership in the fund.

5. YOU SHARE ANY PROFITS

Your shares entitle you to any profits, which can come in three ways:
- Income earned as dividends—even if the fund invests in bonds that earn interest, your payment is still a dividend;
- Capital gains distributed once a year, even though these gains occur any time the manager sells securities from the fund at a profit;
- If you sell shares at a higher price (NAV) than you paid, you will earn a profit. If you sell at a lower price, you will take a loss.

VARIABLE ANNUITIES

The main purpose of a variable annuity is for retirement planning. It has two major parts designed to coincide with the two phases of a person's life: a wealth accumulation phase that coincides with your income-producing years when you're in the best position to accumulate money, and the income management phase, which begins with your retirement years when you need to efficiently manage your income flow to meet your needs. Here's an example of a variable deferred annuity.

WEALTH ACCUMULATION PHASE

BEGIN INVESTING
You can make a one-time, lump sum payment that puts all your money to work immediately or perodic payments that let you add money when you can. Unlike an IRA or 401(k), there is no IRS limit on annual contributions.

CREATE A MIX
You can invest for growth in stock, bond, or cash equivalent products available through the company. You can create a conservative, moderate, or aggressive strategy.

GROW TAX-DEFERRED
Taxes on earnings are postponed until withdrawn. The tax break keeps more of your money working harder to earn even more money.

TRANSFER MONEY TAX-FREE
You can move money among the various investment options without incurring taxes on earnings. Removing this obstacle makes it easier to adjust strategies to meet changing needs.

WITHDRAW MONEY
Earnings can be withdrawn any time. They are taxed as ordinary income. If you're not yet 59 1/2, there may be a 10% IRS penalty. There may also be withdrawal fees, except in catastrophic health cases such as terminal illness or nursing home admission. Any withdrawls will reduce the amount available to work for your retirement needs.

20 There may be fees deducted automatically every year from the annuity account.

TIME TO SMELL ▼ THE FLOWERS
A variable deferred annuity is designed to offer a choice of income streams and help you have more time to stop and smell the flowers.

21 You may have an option to add a death benefit in case you die during the wealth accumulation phase.

INCOME MANAGEMENT PHASE

RETIREMENT

This is the crossover point— the time when you may be ready to receive additional income from the annuity and when you decide how best to use the money you've accumulated. Typically, you can choose from one of the three main payment options shown to the right.

POSTPONE YOUR DECISION

Unlike IRAs and 401(k)s, there are no penalties for failing to take income by age 70, so you can postpone your decision until you're sure what you want to do.

WITHDRAW IT ALL

You can choose to withdraw all of the money at one time and use it as you wish, ending the annuity contract.

SELECT A GUARANTEED INCOME PLAN

You can choose to lock in a guaranteed income plan (*annuitize*). The main options are income for life, for a specific period, or a specific amount for each income payment. If there is a death benefit, it ends here.

MAKE WITHDRAWALS

You can choose to withdraw money at any time and continue to accumulate money. In this case, there is no guaranteed income.

BASIC RISKS OF INVESTING

More than anything else, the fear of risk can turn good investment decisions into bad ones, and even stop people from investing entirely. What's risky for one person may not be risky for someone else. It all depends on one's goals and time frame.

UNDERSTANDING RISK

When you invest, it's important to take the appropriate risk in the context of reaching your goal. If your goal is modest, you can take modest risks. If, however, your goal is challenging, you may face greater risk in getting there but you may also find ways to reduce the risks so they're acceptable.

YOU CAN'T AVOID IT...BUT

The moment you have money—even a paycheck—you face risk. For example, you could cash the check and lose the money. You could put it in a savings account and never earn enough to support yourself in retirement. So understand that even by not investing, you're taking risks.

...YOU CAN WEIGH IT

You always weigh risks with your money, finding the balance and making your choices. For example, you decide whether to buy now or wait for a sale; to save or to spend; to carry a little cash in your wallet or carry a lot.

To find the proper balance in investing, you have to weigh the risks of an investment against the risk of not reaching your goal. Without a goal, you can only assess risk by your emotions.

RISK PERSPECTIVES

The common perspective: The greater the risk, the greater the potential for reward. Another perspective: You can easily increase risk without adding potential for reward. So why do it unless you must to reach your goal?

The common perspective: Certain types of investments are inherently riskier than others. Another perspective: It's how you use the investment. For example, savings accounts are considered to be risk-free, but if you're trying to pay for college tuition, the interest from a savings account will likely leave you short. That's a very big risk.

22 It's not the investment itself that creates the risk. Risk is due mostly to how you choose to use the investment.

...AND CONTROL IT

Just because you invest money somewhere— you let someone else use it—doesn't mean you've lost control. In fact, the financial world is designed specifically to help people control their risks while letting go of their money. It's a heavily regulated world, where new strategies are constantly being created in hopes of lowering risk without harming the potential for profit. As a beginner, you will use a limited number of strategies (explained later in this book) to regulate how fast and far to go in reaching your goals. Advanced investors, though, often combine different kinds of strategies and even different kinds of investments in attempts to control their risks.

...AND USE IT TO YOUR ADVANTAGE

Risk is an essential element in investing that you can use to your advantage. For example, it's common that yields are higher for bonds with higher risk. However, many of those bonds with higher risk aren't risky enough to create problems for most investors. Many accept the higher risk in return for the higher interest they can earn.

23 Asking what the risks are may not be as useful as asking what are the chances of success and failure.

SHORTFALL RISK

S hortfall risk is the risk of not reaching (falling short of) your goal. Make no mistake: This is your biggest investment risk; never lose sight of it. Here's an example of how shortfall risk works when you make investment decisions.

HOW WILL YOU GET THERE?

If you can keep emotions in check, you can look at your goal, where you are now, and how much time you have. Then review the types of investments that have at least the potential to bring you to your goal in time. There is no guarantee that the future will repeat the past, but here's what would have happened to your $5,000 investment from 1980 to 1990.

If you had invested in the stocks of large companies your investment would have grown 17.5% compounded annually to a total of $25,081 in those ten years. You would have reached your goal.

If you had invested in small company stocks your investment would have grown 15.8% compounded annually to $21,680 in the ten years.

If you had invested in long-term corporate bonds your investment would have grown 13.0% compounded annually to $16,973 in those ten years.

If you had invested in Treasury Bonds, your investment would have grown 4.7% compounded annually to $7,915 by 1990.

YOU HAVE **10** YEARS TO

THIS IS WHERE YOU START:

$5,000

24 Visualizing the future you want will help you achieve your goal.

THIS IS WHERE
YOU WANT TO BE:

$25,000

REACH YOUR GOAL OF **$25,000**

BLIND SPOT?

Many financial advisors and personal finance publications don't even mention shortfall risk. One reason why it may be overlooked so often is that the financial industry as a whole is still learning to focus more on you than on investment products.

THE EFFECT OF A SHORTFALL

As the illustration shows, only an investment in large company stocks would have allowed you to reach your goal on time.

The strategies some might consider to be more conservative—bond investments, for example—would have left you falling far from your goal. The farther you fall short, the more you have to do to finance the difference. To fill the gap and reach your goal without taking the appropriate level of risk, you would need to:

- Invest more money each year, so you would have more money earning and compounding for you;
- Finance the shortfall through other means, such as taking cash from the equity in your home, taking another form of loan, or getting other forms of financial assistance (for example, grants and scholarships, if the goal were college tuition). Loans cost money (fees and interest) and those expenses reduce the amount of your wealth.

INFLATION RISK

A nyone with any money needs to understand inflation—
how it affects you and how to protect yourself from it.

> **25** The Consumer Price Index (CPI) measures the change in the cost of goods and services.

WHAT IS INFLATION?

Inflation refers to price increases. But a better word might be disintegration because, like milk that sours and fruit that rots, money is a perishable item that's constantly disintegrating, even though it's difficult for most of us to see. Every year, the value of our money disintegrates at a pace equal to the inflation rate, so that every year your money will buy less than the year before.

If you don't pay attention to inflation, you will never notice how much of your money disappears from year to year, as if simply turning to dust and blowing away

into nothing n e s

AN EXAMPLE

Say you put aside $100 today to buy a $100 coat next year. If prices inflate 3% for the year, the coat will cost $103. It would be as though you simply lost 3% of your money without doing anything.

THE REAL RATE OF RETURN

It's important to know how much your money is earning. But to understand what you will eventually end up with, it's just as important to know how much your money is losing.

THIS IS WHAT'S ▶ EASY TO SEE

You earn a certain amount of interest from an investment. This percentage may be the figure you use to plan your budget for the next year.

THIS IS WHAT'S NOT ▶ SO EASY TO SEE

Your money loses some of its buying power every year. In pre-World War II Germany, inflation was so high, that money would lose almost all of its value literally overnight. People actually found the money more valuable as fireplace kindling.

THIS IS WHAT YOU ▶ ACTUALLY KEEP

Subtracting the percentage lost to inflation from the percentage your money earned, you're actually left with 3.65%. That, in industry terms, is called the real rate of return—a very appropriate name.

TOO MUCH AND TOO LITTLE

Inflation can be caused by having too much money in circulation (high employment can create too much spending money, or the government may be printing a lot of money).

Inflation can also be caused by shortages. If there is a shortage of raw materials or of a product itself, producers may pay higher prices and pass them on to consumers.

MARKET RISK

M arket risk is what keeps some people out of the stock market. It's simply the chance that an investment will lose value after you buy it. What makes market risk particularly intimidating to beginners is that it's unpredictable. Seasoned investors, however, aren't so threatened because while unpredictable, market risk is acceptable, somewhat manageable, and sometimes even desirable—at least temporarily.

HOW IT WORKS

Virtually every investment goes up and down in price—gains and loses value— over time. Prices reflect the public's fears and hopes, affecting supply and demand.

Take a stock for example. If there are many buyers and not enough sellers, the price will rise until it is high enough to induce owners of the stock to sell. If there are too many sellers, the price will eventually drop low enough to where it induces new investors to buy.

Even a stock that's rising steadily may fall in price for at least a day, if there are more investors wanting to sell and take profits than there are new buyers.

FREQUENCY MATTERS

How often and quickly an investment's price can change is called its *price volatility*. Think of it as a sensitivity to market conditions. For example, if a small event causes a price to rise or fall, then it's volatile. If the price stays calm while others move, it's considered stable.

IT CAN BE A ▼ BUMPY RIDE

Investment prices go up and down like a train ride through the mountains. In fact, if you look at a price chart for a stock, it's not hard to imagine it as the track of a train, or even of a rollercoaster.

A price on the rise
This price rise is gradual but they are often steep. A low-quality bond can rise and fall in price as quickly and as sharply as a volatile stock.

A price declining
Here, the price starts a decline. This time it's gradual, but prices can drop sharply.

The price steadies
For a while, the price levels out and the investors' ride is smooth and steady.

WAYS TO MANAGE RISK

Here is what many experts recommend. None of these are hard-and-fast rules.

Don't buy high and sell low. Although it's not a foolproof guarantee, try to avoid buying when a price is historically high or selling when a price is historically low.

Don't jump on bandwagons. Try not to invest in something because everyone you know has already made a profit and you want to profit too. It may be too late.

Pay attention to time. Avoid volatile securities if you:

- Are close to achieving your goals and will soon be ready to sell;
- May need the money for an emergency. Timing is crucial to managing market risk. The key is to avoid situations where you could be forced to sell when prices are down, and therefore, take a loss simply because you had no choice.

Invest for the long-term. Generally speaking, those who plan to stay in an investment for at least five years can ignore the daily ups and downs in prices.

THINGS TO KNOW

- You can get a sense of a stock's price volatility before investing by taking a look at its beta. You can ask your broker or search for it in the stock profile from an online site. Beta measures a stock's volatility compared to the whole market. A beta of 1 means a stock is no more or less sensitive to price changes than the overall market. The higher the number is over 1, the more sensitive the stock. The lower the number is below 1, the less sensitive the stock.

- Many people lose their fear of losing money once they understand that lower prices can be desirable. When the price of an investment is high and then drops, it can create a *buying opportunity*. This means investors think the investment is now cheap enough to make it worth buying—or buying more. It's similar to buying a product on sale for a limited time.

Price movements are unpredictable
On a train, you can look ahead and see the peaks and valleys. Price changes are not as easy to spot.

26 It's not uncommon for a stock price to fluctuate 50% or more during any given year.

INTEREST RATE RISK

C hanges in our economy's interest rates affect the value of many investments, particularly bonds and other fixed income securities. Some inexperienced bond investors don't worry about the value of the bonds they own as long as they continue to earn the interest expected. This lack of concern is fine for anyone committed to holding a bond until maturity (the end of the loan, when the initial investment is repaid in full). For everyone else, however, changes in bond prices are as important as changes in stock prices—and at times they can be just as dramatic.

RATES RISE, PRICES FALL

As rates rise, securities that pay interest tend to fall in price. Most bonds are initially sold for $1,000 (par value) but they may be resold at any time for whatever the investors will pay. If interest rates were to rise, investors would be able to buy newly issued bonds for $1,000 that pay more than your bond. In this scenario, you would have to sell your bond for less than you paid (and take a loss) in order to entice a seller to take it with its lower interest.

HOW RATES AFFECT STOCKS

As interest rates rise, many investors sell some stocks and buy bonds, because they provide more predictability and potential safety. The sell-off in stocks may be slow as rates gradually rise. Some will think that the new interest on bonds is better than owning stocks. Others will wait to see whether rates go higher.

SOME BONDS ARE CALLABLE

Some bonds have a built-in protection clause for the issuers that you should be aware of. The clause says that when interest rates drop, the issuer can *call* the bond, which means they can repay you the $1,000 and end the loan. This is essentially the right to prepay the loan in full without penalty before the due date. Callability gives bond issuers the ability to refinance at lower rates and lower their operational costs, but it creates a risk for investors. They will have to reinvest the money and earn less interest, or pay more to earn the same interest.

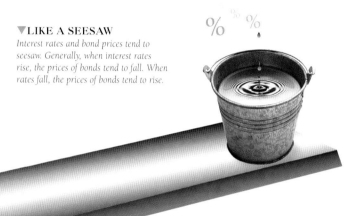

▼LIKE A SEESAW

Interest rates and bond prices tend to seesaw. Generally, when interest rates rise, the prices of bonds tend to fall. When rates fall, the prices of bonds tend to rise.

RATES FALL, PRICES RISE

As interest rates fall, securities that pay interest tend to rise in price. For example, investors must pay $1,000 for a bond with lower interest than a $1,000 bond they could have bought when rates were higher. Now a bond you own with higher interest becomes more valuable. Any investor who wants it must be willing to pay you more than the $1,000 it would cost for a new bond. If you sell at a profit, you add that profit to the interest you've already earned.

27

If you plan to hold a bond to maturity, you can ignore the effects of interest rate risk.

CREDIT RISK

*T*he safety of your investment is subject partly to the creditworthiness of the business or government in which you're investing. This is called credit risk. To assess credit risk, you have to look at your investment the way a lender would look at making a loan to you.

FOR STOCKS

By investing in a company, you are showing faith in its potential success. As a result, you expect its stock price to rise. Part of a company's success may come from its ability to borrow money at good rates when needed. Lenders assess a company's credit the same way they assess yours. In other words, they question the company's:

- Cash, income, and debt to see if it has the financial strength to repay what it borrows;
- History of repayment to see how well it has repaid other loans.

A company's credit rating isn't always readily available to the average investor. But an advisor can help you assess financial strength by looking at the company's annual report.

FOR BONDS

By investing in bonds, you are showing faith in the promises of interest and repayment made to you by the issuer. The safety of your bond investment has a lot to do with the creditworthiness of the company or government standing behind the bond. To assess risk, the bond market relies on independent ratings agencies that continually monitor the financial strength and credit histories of bond issuers. Typically, a bond issuer with:

- Strong credit can borrow money at low rates and still attract investors;
- Poor credit has to offer higher interest rates to attract investors.

28 Just because something is a credit risk doesn't mean it's not worth the investment.

▼ RATINGS SERVICES

The financial world relies heavily on the credit reports issued by the two largest independent ratings services: Moody's and Standard & Poor's. They provide standardized, nationally recognized systems to rate the strength of many bonds issued by corporations and governments. A bond's rating is continually monitored and revised, keeping the investment world informed about the issuer's ongoing level of creditworthiness. Many marketing brochures pitching fixed income mutual funds refer to these ratings. The table below should help you sort out what the ratings mean. You will also find more details on creditworthiness in any fixed income mutual fund prospectus.

JUNK BONDS

Just like people with poor credit, the issuers of junk bonds have poor credit and are therefore less likely to repay their debt as promised. This doesn't automatically translate into a bad investment, however. Many investors are willing to accept the risk in exchange for the higher interest junk bond issuers are willing to pay to attract the money they need.

EXPLANATION	MOODY'S	STANDARD & POOR'S
Bonds of highest quality with the greatest likelihood of repaying in full with interest.	Aaa	AAA
Very strong credit. There's not much difference from the highest rating.	Aa	AA
Still reliable, but may be susceptible to problems in the future.	A	A
Medium-grade. Normally, these are adequate, but have the capacity to weaken in adverse economic conditions.	Baa	BBB
This is the cutoff point for bonds considered "investment grade."		
Bonds with few desirable credit characteristics. Moody's considers them to have speculative aspects.	Ba	BB
Primarily speculative bonds. They carry considerable uncertainty and risk in adverse conditions.	B	B
Highly speculative with poor credit. The lower the rating, the more likely to default.	Caa Ca	CCC CC, C, C1
Lowest rating, usually in default. Little likelihood of being repaid.	C	D

WAYS TO MANAGE RISK

Since risks can't be avoided, a major part of any strategy is to manage the risks involved. Here are some effective strategies for both beginning and advanced investors.

THE ROLE OF TIME

E*verything changes over time. This makes time a critical part of every decision you make about what to do with your money. Whether you buy or sell, lend or borrow, time is a double-edged sword to be used thoughtfully. Time can raise or lower your potential risks and rewards, depending on how you manage it.*

HOW GOALS CHANGE TIME

The risks of time are put into perspective when you have a goal. Without a goal, how can you know what's too long or what's not long enough? When you know how much time you have, your perspective on potential problems changes.

HOW TIME AFFECTS BONDS

In the world of bonds, more time typically means more risk.

Short-term use. If you let go of your money only for short stretches, you reduce the amount of time for something to go wrong. But the less time your money has to work hard, the less money you're likely to earn. With less risk comes less earning potential.

Long-term use. If you let go of your money for long stretches, you lose some control and subject yourself to more risks. But you can earn more because time gives your money more opportunities to grow.

TOO FAST OR TOO SLOW?

If you have far to go in a short time, you will have to go faster. If you have a long time, you can go more slowly. As everyone knows, speeding is usually riskier than going slowly— but not always. Just as slow drivers may never reach their destinations on time, overprotective investors may never reach their goals on time. Look at each potential investment within the context of your goals. Then weigh the likelihood that good things might happen (the potential reward) versus the likelihood that bad things might happen (the risk) within the time you have left.

29 Stocks have outperformed every other type of investment over any ten-year period.

HOW TIME AFFECTS STOCKS

Since as a group stocks carry the most market risk and issues of volatility, it might seem that a long-term investment in stocks would be at greater risk than a short-term investment. But historically, time has tended to make stocks, as a group, one of the lowest risk investments.

Short-term use. If you have short-term goals, short-term rises and drops can look uncomfortably volatile to you. After all, you run the risk of having to sell your stocks and get your money out during a short-term dip in price.

Long-term use. If you have a long-term goal, you can take a broader, calmer, more studied view of the circumstances. You can afford to ride out a short-term roller coaster ride and feel more secure that if stocks continue to repeat their history, the dips will merely seem part of an overall trend that has gone up.

FINE-TUNE CONTROL

Each of these elements can be managed along a spectrum of control, from more control to less, from less trust to greater trust in others.

MANAGEMENT

Do it yourself. Keeping full control of your investments—creating your plan, finding opportunities, making investment decisions, and so forth—is a way to run your investing business on your own. But do-it-yourself investing isn't like building a deck or fixing a water heater. It requires frequent and ongoing maintenance, review, study, and decision making. Be sure you have the time, energy, resources, understanding, and confidence to do it yourself. Otherwise, like any other business, delegate some responsibilities to people who are better at certain tasks than you are. But stay involved as the boss.

Get help. You can get help from books, on-line, discount brokers, full-service brokers, mutual funds, or even hire your own professional money manager. See pages 64-65 for an overview of your options.

LIKE ANYTHING ELSE ▼

Investing can be a do-it-yourself endeavor, just like anything else.

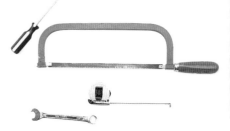

TYPE OF INVESTMENT

The type of investment you select is another way to control your money.

Owning. If you choose to become an owner in a company (stocks), then you are giving up control over that money indefinitely. This means you could take back your money (sell) that same day or many years later. Most importantly, you are letting your money be used any way the company's management wants to use it. So you have to have faith in the business and trust the way the management will run it. Depending upon your percentage of ownership in the company, you may have very little control, if any, over whether or not the company will do well.

Lending. If you choose to lend (buy bonds), then your money will be unavailable for any other use during the time restrictions. In some cases, such as Certificates of Deposit, you agree not to take back the money for the full period. Most bonds, however, have no restrictions. You may sell them whenever you wish. Keep in mind, though, that bond prices fluctuate just as stock prices do, even if with less frequency and degree. So you could decide to sell a bond at a time when the price is less than you paid, and take a loss.

USE OF TIME

Time plays a crucial and constant role in controlling investments .

Short-term. If you can't trust that your money will be used with respect for your needs, or if you expect to need your money soon, then you can invest in a savings account or a money market fund where the money is invested for very short periods (often overnight). These short-term investments don't leave much time for anything to go wrong, and the people using your money take virtually no chances with it. In exchange for the protection, you earn only a little money.

Intermediate term. If you want to earn more, you can allow people to use your money for longer periods (defined by the industry typically as between five and fifteen years). In exchange for the longer time people can use your money, they typically pay more for that privilege. There's also more time for something to go wrong, however, and affect either your ability to get your money or earn what you expect. But in most cases, you can sell your investment to someone else, get some or all of your money back, and let another investor take any further risks.

Long-term. Generally, you can earn the most if you make investments that allow others to use your money for long periods of time. In the case of bonds, that can be as long as thirty years. (You don't have to stay invested that long. You can sell your investment to someone else and let him/her continue with the risks and rewards.) Since your willingness to let your money be used for long periods is usually met with a promise to pay you more for that privilege, the longer-term the bond, the higher the interest tends to be. You're being compensated (even induced) for taking the risks.

USE OF MONEY

Whether you own or lend, the way in which your money will be used is critical to its safety. Who is getting your money and how they plan to use it are both important considerations.

Acceptable use. If you invest in the stock of a very young, aggressive company, for example, you are accepting the fact that your money may be used for very aggressive, high risk purposes, or that the company won't stay competitive and even go out of business. If you invest in a municipal bond and lend your money to a poorly managed city with a low credit rating (a spotty track record of repaying debts), you are also accepting less control. If you invest in a solid entity and/or in a solid use of the money, the reverse is more true. In short, you decide which people and which uses are acceptable or unacceptable to you.

Trust. You have to trust the credit worthiness of the borrower. You also have to assess the soundness of how your money will be used by the borrower.

▲ A DOUBLE-EDGED SWORD
Time can be a double-edged sword, opening more opportunities for positive as well as negative events to occur.

DIVERSIFICATION

H*ow do you know which investments are the right ones? How do you know what's going to happen to the economy? Diversifying your portfolio by spreading your money among a variety of investments that react differently to different events is a simple strategy you can use to manage risk.*

IN STOCKS, YOU CAN DIVERSIFY BY:

GROWTH POTENTIAL AND PRICE STABILITY

- As a well-known quantity, the bigger, well-established companies may not grow dramatically but they may offer the most price stability.
- Mid-sized, established companies may have more room to grow and may also offer less price stability than the big companies.
- Small and start-up companies may offer the most growth potential but are also probably the most likely to be sensitive to price swings.

IN BONDS, YOU CAN DIVERSIFY BY:

BY TYPE OF BOND

To whom do you want to lend your money? The kind of issuer—corporation or government body—can affect the level of investment safety and whether or not income will be taxable. Issuers can be:

- Treasuries (the safest; free from state and local income tax);
- Government bonds (may be free from state and local taxes);
- Municipal bonds (may be free from federal, state, and local income taxes);
- Corporate bonds (taxable).

**DIFFERENT ▶
ANIMALS**
*Stocks and bonds are
different animals.*

HOW YOU EARN MONEY

- Some stocks pay out some profits as dividends, offering regular income.
- Growth stocks reinvest profits to try to keep growing (and keep their stock price growing).
- Some stocks offer both growth and income opportunities.

ECONOMIC CLIMATE

You can try to capture profits in healthy economies and minimize losses in unhealthy market climates by investing money in the global marketplace in:

- Stable, industrialized countries;
- Less-predictable, emerging growth countries.

PRODUCT/SERVICE

What type of industry interests you? There are many industries. Some do better than others in different economic climates.

BY QUALITY

How creditworthy must the borrower be? The credit rating of a bond issue affects the balance between safety and the amount of interest it pays. You can choose:

- High quality bonds usually offer higher safety and lower interest;
- Lower quality bonds usually offer lower safety and higher interest;
- Junk bonds usually offer the lowest safety but the highest interest rate.

BY MATURITY

How long are you willing to lend your money? You can mix the certainty of short-term loans with the higher income of longer-term loans. You can choose:

- Long-term bonds usually offer higher interest rates and the most price volatility;
- Intermediate bonds usually offer mid-range interest rates and mid-range price volatility;
- Short-term bonds usually offer the lowest interest and most price stability.

DOLLAR COST AVERAGING

When is it a good time to invest? What's a good price? You can manage the market risk with an easy strategy called dollar cost averaging.

WHO IS IT FOR?

This most basic of strategies is good for beginners who are resistant to investing, or at least uncomfortable with using their money in a way that they don't fully understand. It's also good for people who can afford to invest only small amounts at a time.

▼ AN EXAMPLE
Below is an example of dollar cost averaging in action. For simplicity, this example excludes all commissions and other costs. All you do is give your broker $500 to invest in the same stock each month no matter what the price.

DAY ONE	DAY 31 (MONTH 2)	DAY 61 (MONTH 3)
The stock price is $5. You invest $500. That buys 100 shares.	*The stock price is now $16.67. You invest $500. That buys 30 shares. Total shares: 130. Your average price per share = $7.69.*	*The stock price is $8. You invest $500. That buys 62 shares. Total shares: 192. Your average price per share = $7.81.*

IT REMOVES THE GUESSWORK

Dollar cost averaging offers you choices. You can invest:

● In stocks, bonds, or mutual funds;
● On a regular schedule automatically;
● Any amount of money you want for each investment.

IT DOESN'T REQUIRE MUCH MONEY

The point is to accumulate a lot of shares over time without using a lot of money each time. Since you're not investing all at once, you don't need to have much money to begin. You may even be able to stick to the plan by transferring money directly from your checking account each month.

30 For many, the purpose of dollar cost averaging is simply to become an investor, even if they only have a little to invest.

A THREE-PART PLAN

There are three parts to dollar cost averaging:
The investment. You select the type of mutual fund, for example, in which to invest;
The timing. You select a regularly scheduled date that coincides with your paycheck (or another logical time);
The amount. You select the amount you feel you can afford to invest at each interval (for example, an amount you might otherwise spend on impulsive purchases you will soon forget).

As the example below shows, you could decide to invest $500 in a mutual fund on the first day of each month. Then you pick a date to make the first investment—and the process begins.

DAY 91 (MONTH 4)

The stock price is up to $9. You invest $500. That buys 55 shares. Total shares: 247. Your average price per share = $8.10.

DAY 121 (MONTH 5)

The stock price is $6. You invest $500. That buys 83 shares. Total shares: 330. Your average price per share = $7.58.

IT'S METHODICAL

Once you begin, you stick with the plan—no matter what happens to the price. Sometimes your money buys more shares; other times, it buys fewer shares.

WHAT IS YOUR PSYCHOLOGY?

If you're buying as the price goes down, will you be the kind of investor who wonders whether you're throwing good money after bad on a poor choice? Or will you trust your initial decision to buy that stock, that the price will rise eventually, and consider yourself lucky to have a chance to buy more shares at bargain prices?

REBALANCING ASSETS

*O*ver time, some of your investments may be stronger performers than others. That tips the balance of your original mix. On a regular basis, it makes sense to review your goals and strategies to see whether you may have to adjust some investments to return the mix to a balance that works best for you.

WHAT REBALANCING IS

Investments change in value all the time, and as they do, they become either a larger or smaller percentage of your overall investment portfolio. To counteract these natural, ongoing shifts in percentages, investors periodically *rebalance* their investment portfolios to the originally intended mix. This enables investors to keep their strategy on course to meet their goals.

HOW REBALANCING WORKS

You sell some of the investments that rose in value, and with that money, buy more of the other kinds of investments that didn't keep pace. There are two ways to rebalance. **Static rebalancing.** This is the strict approach. You set percentages, then regularly return each asset group to that original percentage regardless of market conditions or your outlook for the market. **Tactical rebalancing.** This approach gives you flexibility to shift your target percentages slightly to factor in market conditions and your own outlook. Rather than stick to strict targets, you can shift percentages within an acceptable range.

HOW TO REBALANCE

You simply move some money from the asset group that is above its original percentage into the asset group that is below its original percentage, as the chart below illustrates.

YOU BEGAN WITH:	AFTER A YEAR:	TO REBALANCE:
50% stock funds	65% stock funds	sell 15% of stock funds
30% bond funds	25% bond funds	put 1/3 into bond funds
20% cash equivalents	10% cash equivalents	put 2/3 into cash equivalents

◀ **REBALANCE REGULARLY**
Many experts recommend rebalancing at regular intervals, at least once a year. The frequency depends mainly on how much your investments have changed in value and whether events in your life might cause you to reevaluate your goals and strategy.

THREE BENEFITS

The most important reason to rebalance a portfolio is to keep your strategy on track with your goals. But there are other benefits.

Risk control. It keeps you from taking more risk than you intended. Say, for example, you started with 50% of your money in stock funds, and it grew to 75% of your portfolio. That might be a riskier portfolio than the one you had in mind, especially if the funds you own have a history of higher-than-average market risk (see pages 40-41).

Growth potential. On the other hand, say you started with 50% in stock funds, and it dropped in value to 40% of your portfolio. Now you would have less of your money allocated for growth potential than you first intended. You might sell some of your bond funds and invest the proceeds in the stock funds to again have 50% of your assets there.

Lock in profits. "Buy low, sell high" is one of the cornerstones of successful investing. Therefore, some experts like that rebalancing forces you to sell investments that have gone up in value and buy more of those that have dropped in value. Why? It helps lock in profits from investments that have risen instead of tempting you to try to squeeze out a little more profit by holding investments longer.

UNDERSTANDING PERFORMANCE

Performance—how much money you make—is what investing is all about. There are a number of ways to assess how well your investments are doing in helping you reach your goals.

WHAT YOU EARN

The most obvious way to assess performance is by looking at how much your investments are earning.

TWO TYPES OF EARNINGS

Investments can produce two different types of earnings:

Ordinary income. Bonds pay interest and some stocks pay dividends. These kinds of earnings are considered ordinary income. That's important for tax purposes because dividends and income will be taxed at your usual income tax rate;

Capital gains. If you sell at a higher price than you paid, your profit minus any commissions is a capital gain. Capital gains may be taxed at a lower rate than your usual income tax rate. Consult your tax advisor.

PUMPED PREMIUMS

Generally, bonds are initially sold at $1,000 each, and an investor is repaid $1,000 at maturity (the end of the loan). Sometimes, to give their fund the appearance of high performance, or to give shareholders a temporary high return, mutual fund managers will pay a premium (over $1,000) for bonds with above-average interest. If the fund still holds that bond when it matures, the fund—and you—will take a loss. Say that you're the only shareholder in a fund with only one bond. It cost $1,000 when issued and pays 5% ($50) a year, but when interest rates drop to 4.5%, your fund buys it for $1,100. A year from now, the bond matures and the fund is only paid $1,000. In short, it lost $100, wiping out the $50 in interest you earned for the year, leaving you with an actual loss of $50.

WHEN IS IT EARNINGS?

When your investment goes up in value but you don't sell it, you have *unrealized gains*. The common term for that is *paper profits*, because your profit is only on your statement. Only when you sell at a profit do you make the gain a reality, called a *realized gain* by the industry.

COSTS OF INVESTING

S mart investing means understanding that expenses lower performance. In other words, every penny you pay as a sales charge or other fee will directly reduce your profit. So it makes sense to look at what an investment will cost you, not just at how much it might earn.

STOCKS AND BONDS

There are two main fees for buying and selling stocks and bonds. One is obvious; the other is not so obvious.

Commission. Typically, every time you buy or sell a stock or bond, you pay a commission to your broker. That's easy to see because the amount appears on the order confirmation you receive. With the growth of online trading, brokers are competing for business by aggressively lowering commissions.

The spread. You may think that if you pay a price for a stock, the seller will receive that price as the sales price. That's not how it works. There is something called the *spread*. It's the middleman's profit—the difference between the price a buyer pays and the price the seller receives. The illustration below shows how it works.

MORE IS LESS

STOCK PRICE	THE ASK	THE SPREAD	THE BID	COMMISSION
$20	$20	50¢	$19.50	40¢
You bought one share of stock at $18, and now that the price is $20, you want to sell. It looks like a $2 gain.	The "ask" is the price all buyers pay. But you're selling, not buying. So it's not your price.	This is the profit for the *specialist* who is facilitating trades in that stock. In this case, the spread is 50¢ a share.	This is the price all sellers receive. Since you're a seller, you receive $19.50.	You pay your broker a commission to sell. Let's say it's 20¢ a share. Now you receive $19.30 (you also paid a 20¢ commission to buy, so you're actually down to $19.10).

31 A fund with a 7.5% return and 0.5% in fees will give you a greater net profit than a fund with an 8% return and 1.5% in fees.

Wrap Fees

Some firms charge an annual fee based on the value of your account instead of a commission on each trade. If you trade often, this can save money; if not, you will pay a fee even if you don't trade at all.

Index Funds

The management fee—the fund managers' salaries—is a major expense of a mutual fund. Index funds are unmanaged, because trading occurs based on a computer model that tracks an index (see pages 60-61), not on a manager's subjective decisions. This makes index funds less costly than what are called actively managed funds. That means an index fund doesn't have to perform as well to provide you with the same return on your money.

Portfolio Turnover

Every mutual fund prospectus has a small section called *portfolio turnover*. This tells you how often securities in the fund are bought and sold ("turned over"). The fund pays a commission to its broker every time a trade is made. This expense reduces the fund's—and your— profit. Turnover is shown as a percentage; the higher it is, the higher the expenses.

Mutual Funds

There are different expenses for mutual funds than for stocks and bonds.
Sales charge. Some funds, called *load funds*, charge a commission, called a *sales charge*. No-load funds don't charge a commission. There are also different kinds of sales charges. You may have a choice to pay a sales charge:
● When you buy;
● That reduces each year for a set number of years until there is no sales charge;
● In installments over a few years.
Other fees. There are other fees, as well. Many are annual fees. As a result, no load funds may appear less costly because they have no sales charge, but many have other fees that end up costing you more over time than what the total expenses of some load funds would cost you.

Every mutual fund prospectus now has a simple explanation of expenses and how they may affect your investment over time. Read the fees and expenses sections carefully before investing in any fund.

COMPARING PERFORMANCE

T*he financial industry has developed a tool for comparing your investment's performance against other similar investments. It's called an* index, *which is a measurement of the combined average performance of groups of similar securities.*

TRACKING DEVICES

When you hear that the market went up or went down, you're actually hearing about an index, which is a general indicator of market performance. Here are only some of the many indexes in existence today.

The Dow. The most famous index is the *Dow Jones Industrial Average (DJIA).* It's a formula created (and sometimes revised) by the editors of *The Wall Street Journal.* The Dow tracks the daily gains and losses of thirty stocks from the New York Stock Exchange that the editors consider to be key players in the market and the economy. Right or wrong, their theory is this: As these thirty companies go, so goes the market. Today, experts refer to this as more sentimental than an accurate measure of market performance.

Nasdaq Composite Index. This measures the performance of the entire Nasdaq exchange—over 5,500 stocks. The farther we move into the Information Age, the more this index may become relevant because the majority of Internet and other high tech companies are listed on the Nasdaq.

Large companies. *The Standard & Poor's (S&P) 500 Index* tracks the large stock population. S&P is a financial research and publishing company. This index tracks the daily gains and losses of 500 of the largest U.S. companies (over $5 billion in market value) across a broad range of industries. Tracking many more stocks than the DJIA, the S&P 500 is often referred to by reporters as "the broader market index."

Mid-sized companies. *The S&P MidCap 400* tracks 400 companies ranging in size from $1 billion to $5 billion in market value.

Small companies. *The S&P SmallCap 600* tracks companies from $500,000 to $1 billion in market value. *The Russell 2000* is also a well-followed index, tracking 2,000 small companies, many of them less than three years old.

Bonds. *The Lehman Brothers Aggregate Bond Index* tracks the performance of a combination of certain government bonds, corporate bonds, and mortgage-backed securities.

Risk/return table (Class A shares)

	1 Year	5 Years
Government Securities Fund	12.26%	8.13%
Lehman Long-term T-Bond Index	8.42%	6.99%
Income and Equity Fund	6.79%	9.27%
Lehman Long-term T-Bond Index	8.42%	6.59%
Balanced Fund	1.53%	7.17%
S&P 500 Index	28.59%	24.06%
Lehman Long-term T-Bond Index	8.42%	6.59%
Small Cap Fund	31.40%	8.37%
Russell 2000 Index	7.57%	11.07%

The figures above exclude the sales charge.

Note: Standard & Poor's 500 Index (S&P 500*) is a widely recognized unmanaged index of common stocks. Russell 2000 Index is an unmanaged index of 2,000 small company stocks. Lehman Long-term T-Bond Index is an unmanaged index of long-term government bonds. Unlike the Funds' returns, the total returns of the comparative indexes do not include the effect of brokerage commissions, transaction costs, or other investment costs.

▲ HOW ARE WE DOING?

All mutual funds are required to display easy-to-read comparative tables such as this in their prospectuses.

International stocks. *The Morgan Stanley EAFE Index* is a market-value weighted average of the performance of 1,230 non-U.S. companies representing eighteen stock markets in Europe, Australia, New Zealand, and the Far East.

International Bonds. *The Salomon No U.S. $ World Government Bond Index* is based on the *Salomon Brothers World Bond Index* and excludes bonds issued in U.S. dollars. The index measures the total return of government securities in major sectors of the international bond market, covering approximately 600 bonds across ten currencies.

COMPARE PERFORMANCES

How do you compare the performance of different kinds of investments, such as a bond, a mutual fund, and a stock? You can look at a performance figure called *annual total return*. To see an investment's annual total return, you add:

- The total amount of interest or dividends earned for the year by an investment to the change in price since the beginning of the year;
- Then subtract the annual expenses (which applies to mutual funds) including commissions (which can apply to bonds, stocks, and mutual funds).

All mutual funds have an easy-to-read section in the prospectus that tells you the annual returns for that fund. Using that section, you don't have to do any calculations yourself to compare a variety of different mutual fund investments. You can simply compare the average annual total returns for each fund.

---

32 Use an index to take a quick reading of how the kind of investment you own is doing.

The Effect of Taxes

*T*axes *are a significant part of investing performance because they go right to the bottom line and reduce the amount of earnings you get to keep. They're often overlooked by investors, particularly when considering whether to sell a security and take a profit. Here are the main taxes on investments.*

Ordinary Income

Earnings from stock dividends and bond interest are taxed the same as your salary, at ordinary income tax rates. So the higher your tax bracket the more you will pay out in taxes from your investment earnings.

Capital Gains

When you sell an investment at a higher price than you paid, you're said to have made a capital gain on your investment. This goes for both stocks and bonds since both can appreciate in price from the time of your purchase. Your capital gain would be the difference between what you paid and what you received when you sold an investment, minus any commissions. The tax rate you pay depends on how long you owned the investment. Ask your tax advisor.

Types of Taxable income

Dividends that are interest. Some distributions commonly called dividends are actually interest. You must report these so-called dividends as interest on deposits.

Money market funds. Earnings from money market mutual funds are taxable dividend income. Money market funds are a type of mutual fund. Bank money market accounts, however, pay interest.

Interest on annuities. The accumulated interest on an annuity contract you sell before its maturity date is taxable.

U.S. obligations. Interest on U.S. obligations, such as U.S. Treasury notes and bonds, issued by any agency or instrumentality of the U.S. is federally taxable. It is, however, exempt from state and local taxes.

Dividends on stock sold. If you sell shares of a stock after the dividend is declared but before it's paid, you will receive the dividend and must include it as taxable income.

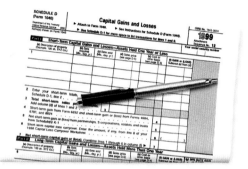

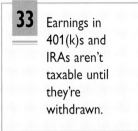

33 Earnings in 401(k)s and IRAs aren't taxable until they're withdrawn.

THINGS TO KNOW

● Many people don't realize that it's common for a mutual fund or a real estate investment trust (REIT) to declare a dividend in October, November, or December, and then pay you in January or February of the next year. These dividends are considered to have been paid to you by December 31, and you're required to report it as income on your tax return that April.

● You never pay taxes on stock gains unless you sell the stock. Therefore, investing for long term helps you save on taxes. That's one reason a long-term view toward investing can go well with a long-term goal.

● Investment income may be subject to backup withholding to ensure that tax is collected on it. The institution holding your account must withhold, as income tax, 31% of the proceeds if you don't provide either a Social Security number or an employer identification number, previously gave an incorrect identification number to the IRS, or underreported interest or dividends on your previous tax return.

CAPITAL LOSSES

If your losses exceed your gains for the year, you can deduct up to $3,000 of those capital losses against your ordinary income and offset them against any capital gains you have, avoiding tax on those gains. If you have any losses left over, you can carry them forward to future years.

34 Municipal bond interest isn't taxable if your home state issued the bond.

STARTING OUT WITH CONFIDENCE

Knowing where to go and who to ask for help when you need it can actually make the investment process easier and may make it more profitable for you.

THE PLAYERS

Think of investing your money as your business. You're creating wealth for yourself. You're the boss of your money. All the people involved work for you.

HOW WILL YOU DIRECT THEM?

As the one in charge of creating wealth for yourself, you have to direct the people you've hired. If you know what you want—if you have clearly established goals—you will have an easier time. The clearer you are about what you want, the easier it will be to pick the right people to help you. They will also be able to do a better job to help you get where you want to be.

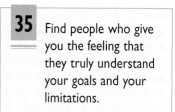

35 Find people who give you the feeling that they truly understand your goals and your limitations.

CAUTION SIGNS

A person who tries to steer you to a particular type of financial product as a planning solution or who regularly tries to sell you something instead of listening to your needs may not be the right financial advisor. In other words, an employee who does more for her- or himself than for your business of creating wealth may not be the right employee for your business.

VISION: FINANCIAL PLANNERS

A financial planner can be an advisor at the highest level of your business. S/he can help you think through your dreams for the future and the goals you want to achieve. S/he can also help you decide what other assistance you might need and help in selecting other professionals to fill those roles.

To fully understand what you want your money to do for you, and what choices are acceptable or unacceptable, the financial planner can become a confidant in intimate aspects of your life. Therefore, it's important to select someone you trust, as well as someone who has solid training in financial planning—not merely in selling investment products.

Financial planners are paid a fee for service or commissions on the products that they sell. A person doesn't need a degree to call himself or herself a financial planner, so be sure to ask for credentials. Certified Financial Planners (CFPs) have to pass a rigorous exam run by a regulatory board.

FULL-SERVICE BROKERS	Full-service brokerage firms vary in what they charge you. Some firms may tempt their employees to recommend certain investments over others.
DISCOUNT BROKERS	These firms take orders and may provide some advice, but you don't have a professional as your consultant. Fees are lower at these firms.
MUTUAL FUND COMPANIES	There are two main types of funds: load funds charge a sales fee; no-load funds don't charge a sales fee. Almost all funds also charge other fees, and some no-load funds are more expensive than some load funds when all fees are considered.
BANKS	All banks offer investments that are aimed at protecting your money. Some offer brokerage services. Be aware that mutual funds through a bank are no safer than those bought through a brokerage firm.
FINANCIAL ADVISORS	Once called brokers, financial advisors help you manage your investments. You pay either an annual fee or commission based on the value of your account.
ONLINE BROKERS	Online brokers can provide information instantly at any hour, with high interactivity and low commissions. Orders aren't necessarily completed faster than through traditional brokers despite the common perception. While uncommon, computer malfunctions could be potentially troublesome.

WHO PROTECTS YOU?

The financial industry is a highly regulated industry. Your best protection is to ask questions and be informed. There are also many rules in place to protect you, and many institutions in place to supervise those rules and assist you when necessary.

36 Every state has some kind of investor protection division.

U.S. SECURITIES AND EXCHANGE COMMISSION

The framework for securities regulation in the U.S. begins with laws passed by Congress. The primary government agency responsible for administering these laws is the *Securities and Exchange Commission (SEC)*. The SEC was established to maintain the integrity of the securities markets and protect investors. To this end, the SEC requires that public companies disclose meaningful financial and other information to investors, providing a common basis for all to judge if a company's securities are a good investment. The SEC also oversees these other key participants in the securities world:

- Broker-dealers;
- Investment advisors;
- Stock exchanges;
- Mutual funds;
- Public utility holding companies.

The SEC has the authority to enforce the laws.

PUBLIC RECORDS

Any investor can access the records of securities professionals and members from the NASD Regulation Public Disclosure Program. Information includes criminal convictions and final disciplinary actions taken by any securities regulator. Check them out online at www.nasd.gov as a place to start.

NATIONAL ASSOCIATION OF SECURITIES DEALERS

The SEC delegates regulatory authority to some private member-owned and operated securities industry organizations. The largest of these self-regulatory organizations is the *National Association of Securities Dealers, Inc. (NASD)*, which has two subsidiaries, NASD Regulation, Inc. and The Nasdaq Stock Market, Inc. For the benefit and protection of investors, the NASD:

● Develops rules and regulations;
● Conducts regulatory reviews of members' business activities;
● Disciplines violators;
● Designs and regulates securities markets and financial services.

FINANCIAL PROFESSIONALS

Securities professionals associated with an NASD member firm must register with the NASD if they sell or supervise the sale of securities to the public. As part of the registration process, NASD Regulation reviews each applicant's employment and disciplinary histories for any evidence that might disqualify him or her from selling securities to the public. S/he must also:

● Be licensed by his or her respective state securities commissions;
● Have his or her fingerprints submitted to the FBI for a criminal record check;
● Pass a series of comprehensive examinations.

37 Every securities firm has an investor complaint department.

38 Many websites provide guidance for investors concerned about fraudulent practices.

READING A STATEMENT

*O*nce you've chosen an investment, you will be receiving a monthly statement of your account. Although statements vary depending on the institution, in general you will find the following information on your monthly statement.

SUMMARY INFORMATION

Total Account Net Worth. This shows the total value of your account at the opening and closing of the statement period (not the value of your account on the day you receive the statement). Some statements have an additional line showing any loans you've taken, appearing in parentheses to indicate that the amount has been subtracted from the value of your securities.

Income and Distributions. Any income earned in your account appears here, both for the statement period and for the entire year up to the closing date of the period.

ACCOUNT ACTIVITY

Every statement offers a detailed chronological listing of every transaction of any kind that occurred during the statement period. By reading this, you can follow the trail of events during the statement period that brought your account from its opening value to its closing value.

Date. This is the date of the transaction.

Transaction. This is the type of transaction.

Quantity. This could be the quantity of the asset or the amount of money involved in the transaction.

Price/Comments. This column may list the price of the security involved in the transaction or offer an explanation about the type of transaction.

Amount Charged/Amount Credited. These two columns show how much was either charged to or earned by your account based on the transaction.

Statement Period

This shows the day coinciding with the opening value and the day that the statement period ended, coinciding with the closing balance.

Securities Account		Prudential Securities Incorporated, a subsidiar

For The Period
September 1 - September 30, 1999

Total Account Net Worth	OPENING	CLOSING	
Priced Securities Value	$33,307.43	$34,268.21	
Money Market Funds	$19.00	$19.00	
Cash Balance	$.88	$.88	
Total Net Worth	$33,327.31	$34,288.09	

Income & Distributions	THIS PERIOD	YEAR TO DATE
Total Income	$.00	$.00

Portfolio Detail

	QUANTITY	CURRENT PRICE
BARON ASSET FUND	29.069	51.570
DREYFUS APPRECIATION FUND INC	26.504	41.970
LAZARD FUNDS INC INTERNATIONAL EQUITY FUND	109.508	16.780
LAZARD FUNDS INC SMALL CAPITAL FUND	86.263	17.520
PRUDENTIAL EQUITY FUND,INC CLASS Z	56.891	19.770
TEMPLETON DEVELOPING MARKETS TRUST CLASS A	49.562	12.340
VAN KAMPEN AGGRESSIVE GROWTH INTERNET 10 (SUBJ TO DEFERRED SALES CHARGE)	614	25.230
VAN KAMPEN HLTH CARE & PHARMACTCL TRST SER 2(SUBJ TO DEFERRED SALES CHARGE)	513.684	8.370
VAN KAMPEN TELECOMMUNICATIONS TR SER 2 (SUBJ TO DEFERRED SALES CHARGE)	522	12.990
PRICED SECURITIES VALUE		

Please see reverse side

THREE MAIN QUESTIONS

All statements are divided into three sections that answer the following basic questions:

- How well was your account doing when the period opened, and where was it when the period closed?
- What took place to cause the change from opening to closing?
- What assets do you own—or, more precisely, what assets did you have in your account at the close of the period?

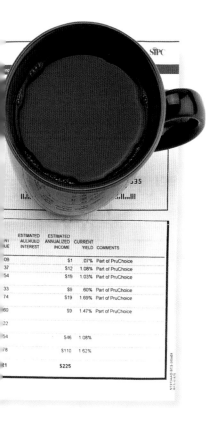

PORTFOLIO DETAILS

This section tells you what assets were in your account at the end of the statement period. Portfolio details can vary widely from statement to statement, depending on how your brokerage firm has organized the information. Most statements, like this one, group all the similar assets (all stocks, all bonds, etc.), then list the assets within each group in alphabetical order.

Quantity. *This tells you how much you own of the asset listed on that line.*

Current Price. *You can see the price of each share of stock, individual bond, mutual fund share, or other single unit of your asset. The figure reflects the price on the last day of the statement period.*

Current Value. *By multiplying the quantity by the current price, you can see the value of the asset on the day the statement period ended.*

Estimated Accrued Interest. *For investments that pay interest, such as bonds, there is an estimate of how much interest you would receive if you sold the investment on the last day of the statement period. The term accrued means that the interest is owed to you even if it hasn't yet been paid into your account.*

Estimated Annualized Income. *This figure shows how much your investment is projected to earn for the entire year in interest, dividends, or both, based on the current payment schedule.*

Current Yield. *If you divide the estimated annualized income by the current value of the asset, you come up with the current yield, also known as the return on your investment, as of the close of the statement period.*

INDEX

loss, 9. See also protecting
   investments; risk management

M

management fees, 59
managing risk. See risk management
market risk, 40–41
market timing, 13
maturity, 23, 51
mid-cap companies, 29
money market funds, 21, 62
monthly statements, 68–69
Moody's, 45
Morgan Stanley EAFE Index, 61
municipal bonds, 25, 63
mutual fund companies, 65
mutual funds, 7, 25, 30–31

N

Nasdaq, 60, 67
NASD Regulation, Inc., 67
National Association of Securities
   Dealers (NASD), 67
Net Asset Value (NAV), 28, 29
no-load funds, 59

O

online brokers, 65
online trading, 13
ordinary income, 56

P

paper profits, 57
par value, 23, 42
performance
   comparing, 60–61
   costs of investing, 58–59
   people involved, 64–65
   taxes and, 62–63
   understanding earnings, 56–57
planning, financial, 10–11
portfolios, 31, 50–51, 54, 59, 69
preferred stock, 29
premiums, 23, 57
prepayment options, 23
price stability, 50
price volatility, 40
principles of investing, 8–11
profits, locked in, 55
protecting investments, 10, 14,
   66–67
publicly held businesses, 26–27
public records, 66

Q

quality of bond issue, 51

R

rate fluctuations, 42–43
rate of return, 39
ratings services, 45
real estate investment trust (REIT), 63
rebalancing assets, 54–55
repricing, 22
retirement planning, 32–33
revenue bonds, 25
rising stock prices, 27
risk
   assessing, 11
   with bonds, 24, 44
   credit, 44–45
   inflation, 38–39
   interest rates, 42–43
   junk bonds, 19, 45
   market, 40–41
   perspectives, 35
   shortfall, 36–37
   taking appropriate, 34–35
risk management
   controlling risk, 34–35, 48–49, 55
   diversification, 50–51
   dollar cost averaging, 52–53
   protection rules, 66–67
   strategies for protecting
   investments, 14
   time factors, 46–47

S

safety of investments, 21, 44–45
sales charges, 59
Salomon No U.S. $ World Gov't
   Bond Index, 61
savings accounts, 21
savings bonds, 24
Securities and Exchange
   Commission (SEC), 66
selling bonds, 22
selling high, 9
share prices, 27
shortfall risk, 36–37
short-term investments, 19, 25, 47, 49
short-term trading, 13
small-cap companies, 29
small company stocks, 18
speculative stocks, 28
spread, 58
stability, price, 50
Standard & Poor's (S&P), 13, 45, 60
statements, 68–69

static rebalancing, 54
stock prices, 29
stocks
   costs of investing, 58
   credit risk of, 44–45
   described, 7
   interest rates, effect of, 42
   long/short-term, 47
   owning, 48
   rising prices, 27
   taxes on gains, 63
   types of, 18, 28–29, 61
strategies. See also protecting
   investments; risk management
   financial planning, 10–11

T

tactical rebalancing, 54
taxable bonds, 25
taxes
   capital gains, 25, 56
   reducing, 17
   tax breaks, 32
   types of on investments, 62–63
time factors, 21, 46–47
timing the market, 13
tracking performance, 60–61
treasury bills, 21, 24

U

undervalued stock, 29
Unit Investment Trusts (UITs), 31
unrealized gains, 57
U.S. government bonds, 24
U.S. obligations, 62
U.S. treasury bills, 21, 24
utilities stocks, 29

V

value stocks, 28
variable annuities, 32–33
volatile stocks, 40

W

wealth accumulation, 32
withdrawals from retirement
   accounts, 32, 33
wrap fees, 59

Y

yield, 23

Z

zero coupon bonds, 24

71

ACKNOWLEDGMENTS

AUTHOR'S ACKNOWLEDGMENTS

The production of this book has called on the skills of many people. I would like particularly
to mention our editors at Dorling Kindersley, and my consultant, Nick Clemente.
Marc wishes to dedicate this book to Bert and Phoebe Robinson for their unending encouragement
and to Zachary Robinson for his great patience and support when it was most needed.

PUBLISHER'S ACKNOWLEDGMENTS

Dorling Kindersley would like to thank everyone who generously lent props for the photoshoots,
and the following for their help and participation:

Editorial Stephanie Rubenstein; **Design and Layout** Hedayat Sandjari; **Preflighting** Mark Schroeder
Consultants Nick Clemente; Skeeter; **Indexer** Rachel Rice; **Proofreader** Stephanie Rose;
Photography Anthony Nex; **Photographers' assistants** Victor Boghassian; Stephanie Fowler;
Models Sandy Crozier; Victor Boghassian; **Picture researchers** Mark Dennis; Sam Ruston.

Special thanks to Teresa Clavasquin for her generous support and assistance.

AUTHOR'S BIOGRAPHY

Marc Robinson is co-founder of Internet-based moneytours.com, a personal finance resource for
corporations, universities, credit unions, and other institutions interested in helping their
constituents make intelligent decisions about their financial lives. He wrote the original
The Wall Street Journal Guide to Understanding Money and Markets, created *The Wall Street Journal
Guide to Understanding Personal Finance*, co-published a personal finance series with Time Life Books, and
wrote a children's book about onomatopoeia in different languages. In his two decades in
the financial services industry, Marc has provided marketing consulting to many top
Wall Street firms. He is admitted to practice law in New York State.